# Dealing with Feeling...
# Worried

Isabel Thomas

## Illustrated by Clare Elsom

Heinemann
LIBRARY

Chicago, Illinois

Edited by Dan Nunn, Rebecca Rissman, and Catherine Veitch
Designed by Philippa Jenkins
Original illustrations © Clare Elsom
Illustrated by Clare Elsom
Production by Victoria Fitzgerald
Originated by Capstone Global Library, Ltd.

**Library of Congress Cataloging-in-Publication Data**
Thomas, Isabel, 1980-
 Worried / Isabel Thomas.
  p. cm.—(Dealing with feeling)
 Includes bibliographical references and index.
 ISBN 978-1-4329-7110-6 (hb)—ISBN 978-1-4329-7119-9 (pb) 1. Worry in children—Juvenile literature. 2. Worry—Juvenile literature. I. Title.
 BF723.W67T56 2013
 152.4'6—dc23          2012008397

Printed in the United States     6035

# Contents

Some words are shown in bold, **like this.** Find out what they mean in the glossary on page 23.

# What Is Worry?

Worry is a **feeling.** It is normal to have many kinds of feelings every day.

Some feelings are not nice to have. Worry is not a nice feeling. We feel worried when we think something bad might happen.

# What Does It Feel Like to Be Worried?

Sometimes we might feel worried for a short time. When you are **nervous**, it can feel like there are butterflies in your stomach.

Sometimes worries can be very strong and last for a long time. It can be difficult to stop thinking about them.

# How Do We Know When Someone Is Worried?

Our faces and bodies can show other people how we are feeling. **Feelings** can change the way that people behave, too.

Some people get grumpy when they are worried, even with their friends. Other people try to hide their worries. This can make them feel worse.

# Is It Normal to Feel Worried?

Some changes are exciting. Others can make you feel worried. It is normal to feel worried about a big change, such as moving to a new house or school.

Take breaks from worrying by doing something you enjoy. There are other things you can do to help yourself feel better, too.

11

# How Can I Deal with Worries?

Sometimes things you see on the Internet or television can make you feel scared. It can be hard to deal with worries on your own.

Ask a grown-up to **explain** what you have seen. Finding out more about something can make it feel less scary.

# Why Is It Good to Share My Worries?

When somebody in your family gets sick, it can make you feel very worried. Talking about your worries can make you feel better.

A grown-up can help you understand what is going on. Sometimes the thoughts inside our heads are very different from what is really happening.

# What If I Can't Talk About My Feelings?

Imagine you are worried because somebody is **bullying** you or your friend. You might be scared that telling a grown-up will make it worse.

Other times, it is hard to put **feelings** into words. Try drawing a picture of your worries instead, and show it to a grown-up whom you trust.

# Why Should I Deal with Worries?

Keeping worries inside can make you feel worse. Worries can get in the way and stop you from enjoying fun things.

You might not be able to **concentrate** in school. The best way to deal with **feelings** is to talk about them.

# How Can I Help Someone Who Is Feeling Worried?

Everyone feels worried sometimes, even grown-ups. When people you know are worried, they might want to talk about how they feel.

You can help by listening. Sometimes, just sharing worries with someone makes the worries go away.

# Make a Worry Toolbox

Write down some tips to help you deal with worried **feelings.**

# Glossary

**bullying**  when a person harms or is nasty to somebody

**concentrate**  focus all your attention on something, so that you can do it well

**explain**  describe something in a way that makes it easier to understand

**feeling**  something that happens inside our minds. It can affect our bodies and the way we behave.

**nervous**  scared or worried about doing something

# Find Out More

## Books

Henkes, Kevin. *Wemberly Worried.*
  New York: Greenwillow, 2010.
Medina, Sarah. *Worried (Feelings).*
  Chicago: Heinemann Library, 2007.
Wolff, Ferida. *Is a Worry Worrying You?*
  Terre Haute, Ind.: Tanglewood, 2007.

## Internet sites

Facthound offers a safe, fun way to find Internet sites related to this book. All of the sites on Facthound have been researched by our staff.

Here's all you do:
Visit www.facthound.com
Type in this code: 9781432971106

# Index

# Dealing with Feeling...
# Angry

Isabel Thomas

Illustrated by Clare Elsom

Heinemann LIBRARY

Chicago, Illinois

Edited by Dan Nunn, Rebecca Rissman, and
 Catherine Veitch
Designed by Philippa Jenkins
Original illustrations © Clare Elsom
Illustrated by Clare Elsom
Production by Victoria Fitzgerald
Originated by Capstone Global Library, Ltd.

**Library of Congress Cataloging-in-Publication
Data**
Thomas, Isabel, 1980-
 Angry / Isabel Thomas.
   p. cm.—(Dealing with feeling)
 Includes bibliographical references and index.
 ISBN 978-1-4329-7103-8 (hb)—ISBN 978-1-4329-
7112-0 (pb)  1. Anger in children—Juvenile literature.
2. Anger—Juvenile literature.  I. Title.
 BF723.A4T56 2013
 152.4'7—dc23          2012008275

# Contents

Some words are shown in bold, **like this**. Find out what they mean in the glossary on page 23.

# What Is Anger?

Anger is a **feeling**. It is normal to have many kinds of feelings every day.

Everyone feels angry sometimes. We might feel angry when something hurts us, annoys us, or seems unfair.

# How Do We Know When Someone Is Angry?

Our faces and bodies can show other people how we feel inside. **Feelings** can change the way that people behave, too.

Some people get quiet or cry when they are angry. Other people may shout, or try to hurt people or break things.

# What Does Anger Feel Like?

Anger can make you feel hot and shaky inside. You might feel as if the anger is trapped inside your body, waiting to burst out.

It can be easy to get angry. It can be harder to stop being angry. Trying to hide angry **feelings** can make you feel worse.

# Is It Okay to Feel Angry?

When somebody else breaks the rules, it can make you lose your temper. Many people feel angry when something is unfair.

It is okay to feel angry, but it is not okay to hurt people. You need to find a safe way to let anger out.

# How Can I Deal with Anger?

Getting in trouble for something that you did not do can make you feel angry. It is okay to feel angry, but it is not okay to shout at people.

The best way to deal with **feelings** is to talk about them. You could tell the person who made you angry how you feel.

# What If I Am Too Angry to Talk?

When someone makes fun of you, it can make you feel upset. It is okay to feel angry, but it is not okay to **damage** other people's things.

Find a safe way to let your anger out. You could scribble on scrap paper or tear up old newspaper.

# What Are Safe Ways to Let Anger Out?

It can be **frustrating** to not be the winner. It is okay to feel bad, but it is not okay to punch, kick, or throw things.

Exercise is a safe way to let anger out. You could go for a run or a walk, or jump up and down.

# How Can I Help Myself Calm Down?

When something you have made gets broken, you might feel angry. It is okay to feel grumpy, but it is not okay to fight.

Calm down by walking away. Try taking ten deep breaths. You could drink a glass of water to cool yourself down.

19

# How Can I Help Someone Else Who Is Angry?

Everyone feels angry sometimes, even grown-ups. Sometimes angry people are not nice to other people, because they are feeling bad inside.

When they calm down, they might want to talk about how they feel. You can help by listening.

# Make an Anger Toolbox

Write down some tips to help you deal with angry **feelings.**

# Glossary

**damage** do harm to something

**feeling** something that happens inside our minds. It can affect our bodies and the way we behave.

**frustrating** something that makes us feel upset or annoyed because we cannot change it

# Find Out More

## Books

Bang, Molly. *When Sophie Gets Angry—Really, Really Angry*. New York: Scholastic, 2007.

Bingham, Jane. *Angry (Everybody Feels)*. New York: Crabtree, 2008.

## Internet sites

Facthound offers a safe, fun way to find Internet sites related to this book. All of the sites on Facthound have been researched by our staff.

Here's all you do:
Visit www.facthound.com
Type in this code: 9781432971038

# Index

# Dealing with Feeling...
# Caring

Isabel Thomas

Illustrated by Clare Elsom

Heinemann LIBRARY

Chicago, Illinois

© 2013 Heinemann Library
an imprint of Capstone Global Library, LLC
Chicago, Illinois

To contact Capstone Global Library please
phone 800-747-4992, or visit our website
www.capstonepub.com

Edited by Dan Nunn, Rebecca Rissman, and
 Catherine Veitch
Designed by Philippa Jenkins
Original illustrations © Clare Elsom
Illustrated by Clare Elsom
Production by Victoria Fitzgerald
Originated by Capstone Global Library, Ltd.

**Library of Congress Cataloging-in-Publication
Data**
Thomas, Isabel, 1980-
  Caring / Isabel Thomas.
     p. cm.—(Dealing with feeling)
  Includes bibliographical references and index.
  ISBN 978-1-4329-7104-5 (hb)—ISBN 978-1-
4329-7113-7 (pb)  1. Caring in children—Juvenile
literature. 2. Caring—Juvenile literature.  I. Title.
  BF723.C25T56 2013
  177'.7—dc23          2012008276

Printed in the United States        6035

# Contents

Some words are shown in bold, **like this.** Find out what they mean in the glossary on page 23.

# What Does Being Caring Mean?

Everybody has **feelings**. Being caring means that you care about other people's feelings.

Caring people like to help other people feel good. They are being caring when they help others.

# What Does It Feel Like to Be Caring?

Caring people feel bad when someone else is sad, angry, worried, or lonely. They try to help people feel better.

Helping people feel good makes you feel good, too. Being caring also helps you make new friends.

# How Can I Be Caring?

You can be caring every day. Look for ways to help other people.

Caring people know when things are
fair or unfair. They do their best to
make things fair.

# How Do Rules Help Me to Be Caring?

A caring person knows that rules help to make things fair for everyone. You can be caring by **obeying** rules.

You can be caring by helping with **housework**, even when it is not your turn. Being caring means putting other people before yourself.

# How Can I Help My Friends to Feel Happy?

What do you do when your friends are sad or worried? Caring people make time to listen to their friends.

Be a good listener by asking questions. Look at people when they speak and don't **interrupt.**

# How Can I Help Other People to Feel Happy?

**Imagine** that a new child joins your class. The child might be sad, scared, or shy.

You can be caring by speaking to the new child. A caring person makes sure nobody feels left out.

# What If I Get Mad at Someone?

It is okay to feel angry sometimes. Thinking about how the other person feels will make you feel better. Perhaps the person did not mean to upset you.

Caring people say sorry when they have been unkind to somebody. Being caring means being **forgiving.**

# What Should I Do If Someone Is Not Being Caring?

Being caring means doing the right thing. If you see someone being unkind, the right thing to do is to tell a grown-up.

You can help by being kind to children who have been **bullied**. A caring person does not tease or bully people.

# How Can Being Caring Make Me Happy?

Caring people are good friends to have. They are there when you need them.

If you are caring and helpful, people
will share things with you. Being a
good friend will help make you feel
happy, too!

# Make a Caring Toolbox

Write down some tips to help you care for others.

Notice when someone else is sad, mad, worried, or lonely.

**Be a good listener.**

Put other people before yourself.

**Tell a grown-up if you see someone being unkind.**

Include other people in your games.

**Be friendly to children you don't know.**

Look for ways to help people.

**Share and wait your turn.**

# Glossary

**bullied** to be harmed or made fun of by somebody

**feeling** something that happens inside our minds. It can affect our bodies and the way we behave.

**forgiving** stop being angry with someone who has upset you

**housework** jobs that need to be done around your home

**imagine** make a picture in your head

**interrupt** stop somebody who is speaking by starting to speak yourself

**obeying** doing what a rule or grown-up says you are supposed to do

# Find Out More

## Books

Raatma, Lucia. *Caring* (21st Century Junior Library). Ann Arbor, Mich.: Cherry Lake, 2009.

Stead, Philip. *A Sick Day for Amos McGee*. New York: Roaring Brook, 2010.

## Internet sites

Facthound offers a safe, fun way to find Internet sites related to this book. All of the sites on Facthound have been researched by our staff.

Here's all you do:
Visit www.facthound.com
Type in this code: 9781432971045

# Index

# Dealing with Feeling...
# Happy

Isabel Thomas

Illustrated by Clare Elsom

Heinemann LIBRARY

Chicago, Illinois

Edited by Dan Nunn, Rebecca Rissman, and Catherine Veitch
Designed by Philippa Jenkins
Original illustrations © Clare Elsom
Illustrated by Clare Elsom
Production by Victoria Fitzgerald
Originated by Capstone Global Library, Ltd.

**Library of Congress Cataloging-in-Publication Data**
Thomas, Isabel, 1980-
  Happy / Isabel Thomas.
      p. cm.—(Dealing with feeling)
  Includes bibliographical references and index.
  ISBN 978-1-4329-7105-2 (hb)—ISBN 978-1-4329-7114-4 (pb)  1. Happiness in children—Juvenile literature. 2. Happiness—Juvenile literature.  I. Title.
  BF723.H37T56 2013
  152.4'2—dc23          2012008277

Printed in the United States     6367

# Contents

Some words are shown in bold, **like this.** Find out what they mean in the glossary on page 23.

# What Is Happiness?

Happiness is a **feeling**. It is normal to have many kinds of feelings every day.

Some feelings are nice to have. Happiness is a nice feeling. You can help yourself to feel happy more often.

# How Does It Feel to Be Happy?

When we are happy, we feel good about ourselves. Smiling or laughing shows other people how we feel.

6

Being happy makes us feel brave or **confident.** It helps us to do the things that we want to do.

# What Makes People Happy?

Sometimes other people do things to make us happy, such as giving us a surprise present. We can also do things to make ourselves happy.

Many people feel happy if they do well at something. You can make yourself happy by working hard to do well in school and at home.

# What Can I Do to Feel Happy?

Being around other people can make us feel happy. Talking and playing with friends and family is fun.

You can make new friends by smiling and saying, "Hello." Meet new people by playing sports or starting a new **hobby** outside school.

# What If I Am Feeling Sad?

Everyone feels sad sometimes. Talking to someone can make you feel happier.

12

You can cheer yourself up by doing something you enjoy. Try reading a book or watching a funny movie.

# How Can I Turn Sad Feelings into Happy Ones?

**Feelings** can change the way that people behave. What do you do when something makes you feel angry, sad, or **jealous**?

If you think happy thoughts it will help you to feel better. If you are cheerful and kind, people will do things to make you happy, too!

# What Is the Quickest Way to Feel Happy?

Try frowning, then smiling. How do you feel inside? You can make yourself feel happier just by smiling!

Smiling makes other people feel friendly toward you, too. Who would you most like to be friends with in this picture?

# What If I Have to Do Something I Don't Like Doing?

How do you feel when you are asked to clean up at school or at home? If people ask for your help, it means they think you will do a good job.

When you have finished, you will feel **proud**. The person you helped will be pleased. Helping other people can make YOU feel happy, too!

# How Can I Make Other People Feel Happy?

Nobody feels happy all the time. Your friends and family might feel sad, angry, or worried sometimes.

They might want to talk about how they feel. You can help them to feel happier by listening and by being a good friend.

# Make a Happiness Toolbox

Write down some tips to help you feel happy every day.

Set yourself a goal and work hard to do well at it.

Find a friend or family member to talk to.

Smile!

Read a book or watch a movie that you enjoy.

Go for a walk or a run outside.

If you feel sad, try doing something different.

Make others happy by helping them.

Learn a new **hobby** or sport.

Don't be afraid to ask for help. Everyone needs help sometimes.

# Glossary

**confident** feeling that you can do something well

**feeling** something that happens inside our minds. It can affect our bodies and the way we behave.

**hobby** activity that you do for fun, in your own time

**jealous** feeling upset or grumpy that you do not have something that another person has

**proud** feeling pleased with yourself

# Find Out More

## Books

Bingham, Jane. *Happy (Everybody Feels)*.
  New York: Crabtree, 2008.
Carlson, Nancy. *Smile a Lot!* Lerner, 2012
Medina, Sarah. *Happy (Feelings)*.
  Chicago: Heinemann Library, 2007.

## Internet sites

Facthound offers a safe, fun way to find Internet sites related to this book. All of the sites on Facthound have been researched by our staff.

Here's all you do:
Visit www.facthound.com
Type in this code: 9781432971052

# Index

# Dealing with Feeling....
# Jealous

Isabel Thomas

Illustrated by Clare Elsom

Heinemann
LIBRARY

Chicago, Illinois

Edited by Dan Nunn, Rebecca Rissman, and
  Catherine Veitch
Designed by Philippa Jenkins
Original illustrations © Clare Elsom
Illustrated by Clare Elsom
Production by Victoria Fitzgerald
Originated by Capstone Global Library, Ltd.

**Library of Congress Cataloging-in-Publication
Data**
Thomas, Isabel, 1980-
 Jealous / Isabel Thomas.
   p. cm.—(Dealing with feeling)
 Includes bibliographical references and index.
 ISBN 978-1-4329-7106-9 (hb)—ISBN 978-1-
4329-7115-1 (pb) 1. Jealousy in children—Juvenile
literature. 2. Jealousy—Juvenile literature.  I. Title.
 BF723.J4T56 2013
 152.4'8—dc23          2012008278

# Contents

Some words are shown in bold, **like this**. Find out what they mean in the glossary on page 23.

# What Is Jealousy?

Jealousy is a **feeling**. It is normal to have many kinds of feelings every day.

Everyone feels jealous sometimes.
You might feel jealous if you think
someone else is better than you, or
if someone has something you want.

# How Do We Know When Someone Is Feeling Jealous?

Our faces and bodies can show other people how we are feeling. **Feelings** can change the way that people behave, too.

Some people may become quiet and sad when they feel jealous. Others may behave badly, even toward their friends and family.

# What Does Jealousy Feel Like?

Jealousy can make you feel sad or grumpy that you do not have what other people have.

You might not feel like being nice to people. Trying to hide jealous **feelings** can make you feel worse.

# Is It Okay to Feel Jealous?

If your best friend starts playing with new friends, it can make you feel jealous. You might feel sad or angry and say nasty things.

It is okay to feel jealous, but it is not okay to be unkind to somebody. You can learn to deal with jealous **feelings** and be a good friend.

# How Can I Deal with Jealousy?

Sometimes jealous **feelings** start because you are worried about something. You might feel worried that your parents do not have enough time to play with you anymore.

The best way to deal with feelings is to talk about them. Share your feelings with your parents or friends. They can help you to feel less jealous.

# Why Should I Deal with Jealous Feelings?

Jealousy can make you feel that you are not as good as other people. It can make you behave **unkindly.**

It is okay to feel jealous, but it is
not okay to tease somebody or to
say nasty things about a person.
This will make you feel worse.

# What Should I Do When I Feel Jealous of Something?

When someone has something you want, it can make you feel jealous. You might want to take what the person has to make things seem fair.

It is okay to feel jealous, but it is not okay to take or break someone's **property**. Deal with jealous **feelings** by doing something that makes you happy.

# What Should I Do When I Feel Jealous of Somebody?

Jealousy can make you feel unhappy when someone else does well. You might feel that you are not good enough.

It is normal to want to do well. Try to be happy when someone else does well, too. Be friendly and say, "Great job!"

# How Can I Help Someone Who Is Feeling Jealous?

Remember that everybody feels jealous sometimes. If you notice someone who is feeling jealous, you can help the person feel better.

When you make new friends, remember to be kind to your old friends, too. Share what you have with other people, and they will share things with you.

# Make a Jealousy Toolbox

Write down some tips to help you deal with jealous **feelings.**

If someone does something well, say, "Great job!"

Remember that everyone is different. Our differences make us special.

Think about all the things that make you happy.

Remember that you can always feel proud if you have done your best.

Do something you enjoy.

Try not to compare yourself to other people.

Remember that you will get better if you keep trying at something.

Remember all the things you are good at.

# Glossary

**feeling** something that happens inside our minds. It can affect our bodies and the way we behave.

**property** something that belongs to someone

**unkindly** in a nasty way. Being unkind to someone can make the person feel sad.

# Find Out More

### Books

Kravetz, Jonathan. *How to Deal with Jealousy (Let's Work It Out)*. New York: PowerKids, 2007.

Medina, Sarah. *Jealous (Feelings)*. Chicago: Heinemann Library, 2007.

### Internet sites

Facthound offers a safe, fun way to find Internet sites related to this book. All of the sites on Facthound have been researched by our staff.

Here's all you do:
Visit www.facthound.com
Type in this code: 9781432971069

# Index

# Dealing with Feeling...
# Proud

Isabel Thomas

Illustrated by Clare Elsom

LIBRARY

Chicago, Illinois

© 2013 Heinemann Library
an imprint of Capstone Global Library, LLC
Chicago, Illinois

Edited by Dan Nunn, Rebecca Rissman, and Catherine Veitch
Designed by Philippa Jenkins
Original illustrations © Clare Elsom
Illustrated by Clare Elsom
Production by Victoria Fitzgerald
Originated by Capstone Global Library, Ltd.

**Library of Congress Cataloging-in-Publication Data**
Thomas, Isabel, 1980-
  Proud / Isabel Thomas.
      p. cm.—(Dealing with feeling)
  Includes bibliographical references and index.
  ISBN 978-1-4329-7107-6 (hb)—ISBN 978-1-4329-7116-8 (pb)  1. Self-esteem in children—Juvenile literature. 2. Self-esteem—Juvenile literature. 3. Pride and vanity—Juvenile literature.  I. Title.
  BF723.S3T56 2013
  152.4—dc23            2012008394

Every effort has been made to contact copyright holders of material reproduced in this book. Any omissions will be rectified in subsequent printings if notice is given to the publisher.

All the Internet addresses (URLs) given in this book were valid at the time of going to press. However, due to the dynamic nature of the Internet, some addresses may have changed, or sites may have changed or ceased to exist since publication. While the author and publisher regret any inconvenience this may cause readers, no responsibility for any such changes can be accepted by either the author or the publisher.

Printed in the United States    6035

# Contents

Some words are shown in bold, **like this.** Find out what they mean in the glossary on page 23.

# What Is Pride?

Pride is a **feeling**. It is normal to have many kinds of feelings every day.

4

Some feelings are nice to have. Pride is a nice feeling. We feel proud when we are pleased with ourselves.

# What Makes People Feel Proud?

When somebody says that we are kind or look good, we feel proud. It is nice to get a **compliment**.

6

We feel proud when we do something well or achieve a goal. We feel proud when we are brave and do something that scares us.

# What Does Pride Feel Like?

When you are proud, you feel good about yourself.

You might feel more **confident.**
Pride can make you want to work
hard and do well again.

# How Can Pride Make Other People Feel?

People show their **feelings** in different ways. Feeling proud can make us act like we are more important than other people.

It might look as if we are **showing off**. This can make other people feel jealous, angry, or sad.

# What If Other People Do Not Seem Pleased for Me?

It is normal to feel proud when you do something well. It can be hard when other people do not seem pleased for you.

Remember that they have **feelings,** too. They might feel sad that they are not the best this time.

# How Should I Deal with Pride?

Sometimes we feel proud because we have something that other people **admire**. It is nice to feel proud. It is not nice to **boast** about what you have.

14

When you feel proud, remember not to **show off.** You can be a good friend by sharing what you have.

# What If I Have Nothing to Feel Proud About?

Everyone has something to feel proud about. Ask your friends why they like hanging out with you.

Ask your family what they like most about you. You can be proud of being a great brother or sister, a great son or daughter, or a great friend.

# What Can I Do to Feel Proud?

You can feel proud by working hard in school. You can feel proud when you help out at home.

18

You do not have to BE *the* best to be proud of yourself. You just have to DO your best.

# How Can I Help Other People to Feel Proud?

You can make people feel proud by giving them **compliments**. It is nice to make other people feel good about themselves.

If you are good at doing something, try teaching other people how to do it. Everyone feels proud when they learn something new.

21

# Make a Pride Toolbox

Write down some tips to help you feel proud every day.

Talk about how you have helped other people.

Think about how you help out around your home.

What things are you good at in school?

Keep a note of praise you get at school or at home.

List some new skills that you have learned.

Remember nice things people have said about you.

Think of what makes you a good friend.

Think of times that you have been brave.

# Glossary

**admire**  think that something is good

**boast**  talk about things that you have or can do in a way that makes other people feel bad

**compliment**  when you tell somebody something that you like about him or her

**confident**  feeling that you can do something well

**feeling**  something that happens inside our minds. It can affect our bodies and the way we behave.

**show off**  boast about things that you have or can do

# Find Out More

## Books

Ludwig, Trudy. *Better Than You.* Berkeley: Tricycle, 2011.

Medina, Sarah. *Proud (Feelings).* Chicago: Heinemann Library, 2007.

## Internet sites

Facthound offers a safe, fun way to find Internet sites related to this book. All of the sites on Facthound have been researched by our staff.

Here's all you do:
Visit www.facthound.com
Type in this code: 9781432971076

# Index

# Dealing with Feeling...
# Shy

Isabel Thomas

Illustrated by Clare Elsom

Chicago, Illinois

© 2013 Heinemann Library
an imprint of Capstone Global Library, LLC
Chicago, Illinois

Edited by Dan Nunn, Rebecca Rissman, and
  Catherine Veitch
Designed by Philippa Jenkins
Original illustrations © Clare Elsom
Illustrated by Clare Elsom
Production by Victoria Fitzgerald
Originated by Capstone Global Library, Ltd.

**Library of Congress Cataloging-in-Publication
Data**
Thomas, Isabel, 1980-
  Shy / Isabel Thomas.
    p. cm.—(Dealing with feeling)
  Includes bibliographical references and index.
  ISBN 978-1-4329-7109-0 (hb)—ISBN 978-1-4329-
7118-2 (pb)  1. Bashfulness in children—Juvenile
literature. 2. Bashfulness—Juvenile literature.  I. Title.
  BF723.B3T56 2013
  155.2'32—dc23          2012008396

All the Internet addresses (URLs) given in this book
were valid at the time of going to press. However,
due to the dynamic nature of the Internet, some
addresses may have changed, or sites may have
changed or ceased to exist since publication. While
the author and publisher regret any inconvenience
this may cause readers, no responsibility for any such
changes can be accepted by either the author or
the publisher.

# Contents

Some words are shown in bold, **like this**. Find out what they mean in the glossary on page 23.

# What Is Shyness?

Shyness is a **feeling**. It is normal to have many kinds of feelings every day.

Some feelings are not nice to have. Shyness is not a nice feeling. We might feel shy when we try new things or speak in front of people.

5

# How Do We Know When Someone Is Feeling Shy?

Our faces and bodies can show other people how we are feeling. Some people may speak quietly when they are feeling shy.

Other people may not speak at all. Sometimes people might look unfriendly, when really they are just feeling shy.

7

# What Does It Feel Like to Be Shy?

Shyness can make us feel a little scared around other people. We might worry about doing something **embarrassing**.

Shyness can mean we do not say
or do the things we would like to.
Being left out can make us feel
badly about ourselves.

# Is It Normal to Feel Shy?

Sometimes we might feel shy for a short time. It is normal to feel shy when you do something for the first time.

Take time to get used to a new **activity.** Watch other people and see how they act. This will help you to feel more **confident.**

# How Can I Deal with Shyness?

Many people feel shy when they meet new people for the first time. You might feel that you do not know what to say.

The best thing to do when you feel shy is to smile. A shy face may look scared or grumpy. A smiling face always looks friendly.

# How Do I Start Talking to New People?

A big change, such as starting a new school, can be scary. You might feel shy because you do not know what the children and teachers will be like.

A good way to make new friends is to ask people questions about themselves. Maybe you like the same books or computer games!

# How Can I Get Better at Talking in Front of People?

Many people feel **nervous** when they have to speak in front of lots of people. This might make you too shy to raise your hand in class.

Practice reading out loud to your family or friends. The more you practice speaking to a group, the easier it will get.

# What If I Feel Shy All the Time?

Sometimes shy **feelings** can be very strong and stop us from doing things we enjoy. You might feel shy if how you look or the things you do make you different from other people.

18

The best way to deal with shy feelings is to talk about them. Share your worries with others. They might tell you what they do to feel less shy.

# How Can I Help Someone Who Is Feeling Shy?

Everyone feels shy sometimes. Ask your friends, teachers, or parents what makes them feel shy.

The next time you spot people who are not joining in, remember that they might be feeling shy. Help them to make friends by being friendly yourself.

21

# Make a Shyness Toolbox

## Write down some tips to help you deal with shy **feelings.**

Practice doing new things with your friends or family.

Relax and take deep breaths to keep your body calm.

Give yourself a treat every time you try something new.

Give someone a **compliment.** This is a good way to start talking to someone new.

Talk about your feelings with someone you trust.

Don't be afraid to ask for help. Everyone needs help sometimes.

Ask people questions about themselves.

Smile! A smiling face always looks friendly.

# Glossary

**activity**  something you do for fun

**compliment**  something nice that you say about someone

**confident**  feeling that you can do something well

**embarrassing**  something that makes you feel awkward, as if you have done something wrong

**feeling**  something that happens inside our minds. It can affect our bodies and the way we behave.

**nervous**  scared or worried about doing something

# Find Out More

## Books

Medina, Sarah. *Shy (Feelings)*.
Chicago: Heinemann Library, 2008.
Twohy, Mike. *Poindexter Makes a Friend*. New York:
Simon & Schuster, 2011.

## Internet sites

Facthound offers a safe, fun way to find Internet sites related to this book. All of the sites on Facthound have been researched by our staff.

Here's all you do:
Visit www.facthound.com
Type in this code: 9781432971090

# Index

# Dealing with Feeling...
# Sad

Isabel Thomas

Illustrated by Clare Elsom

Heinemann LIBRARY

Chicago, Illinois

© 2013 Heinemann Library
an imprint of Capstone Global Library, LLC
Chicago, Illinois

Edited by Dan Nunn, Rebecca Rissman, and Catherine Veitch
Designed by Philippa Jenkins
Original illustrations © Clare Elsom
Illustrated by Clare Elsom
Production by Victoria Fitzgerald
Originated by Capstone Global Library, Ltd.

**Library of Congress Cataloging-in-Publication Data**

Thomas, Isabel, 1980-
  Sad / Isabel Thomas.
    p. cm.—(Dealing with feeling)
  Includes bibliographical references and index.
  ISBN 978-1-4329-7108-3 (hb)—ISBN 978-1-4329-7117-5 (pb)  1. Sadness in children—Juvenile literature. 2. Sadness—Juvenile literature.  I. Title.
  BF723.S15T56 2013
  152.4—dc23            2012008395

Printed in the United States    5920

# Contents

Some words are shown in bold, **like this.** Find out what they mean in the glossary on page 23.

# What Is Sadness?

proud

jealous

happy

angry

Sadness is a **feeling.** It is normal to have many kinds of feelings every day.

4

Some feelings are not nice to have. Sadness is not a nice feeling. We might feel sad when something bad happens, or because we are lonely or scared.

5

# How Do We Know When Someone Is Sad?

Our faces and bodies can show other people how we are feeling. How do you show other people that you are feeling sad?

Not everyone shows sadness in the same way. Some people may cry when they are sad. Others may try to hide their sad **feelings** or be grumpy, even with their friends.

# What Does It Feel Like to Be Sad?

Sadness can make you feel like there is nothing to look forward to. You might stop enjoying things that are usually fun.

Sometimes sad **feelings** can be very strong. You might not be able to **concentrate** in school.

# Is It Okay to Feel Sad?

FUNFAIR
TODAY

It is okay to feel **disappointed** when something does not work out. Trying to hide sad **feelings** can make you feel worse.

Crying can make you feel better. It lets the sad feelings out. There are other things you can do to help yourself feel better, too.

# How Can I Deal with Sadness?

Being left out can make you feel lonely. It is normal to feel sad when you cannot join in with your friends.

The best way to deal with **feelings** is to talk about them. Share your problems with your friends and family. They can help you to find **solutions**.

# How Else Can I Share My Feelings?

Everyone feels sad when they miss somebody. Sometimes you cannot be with the person you want to talk to the most.

You can show your **feelings** in other ways. Write a letter or paint a picture telling the person how much you love him or her.

# What If Somebody Else Is Making Me Feel Sad?

It is wrong to make fun of people because of the way they look or the things they do. Being **teased** can make people feel very sad.

If someone teases or **bullies** you, do not hide your sad **feelings**. Tell a grown-up. Grown-ups can help you solve the problem.

# What If I Never Feel Happy Again?

If we fall over and hurt ourselves we might feel unhappy for a short time. But if something very sad happens as when a pet dies, then the sad **feeling** can be very strong.

Your sad feelings will not last forever. You can help yourself feel better by talking to someone.

# How Can I Help Someone Who Is Feeling Sad?

Everyone feels sad sometimes—even grown-ups. Some people want to be alone when they are sad.

Other people like to have a friend to **comfort** them. They might want to talk about how they feel. You can help by listening.

# Make a Sadness Toolbox

Write down some tips to help you deal with sad **feelings**.

# Glossary

**bully** when a person harms or is nasty to somebody

**comfort** try to make people feel less sad by talking to them and being there for them

**concentrate** focus all your attention on something

**disappointed** sad because something did not turn out how you thought it would

**feeling** something that happens inside our minds. It can affect our bodies and the way we behave.

**solution** way of fixing problems

**teased** be made fun of

# Find Out More

## Books

Bingham, Jane. Sad (Everybody Feels).
   New York: Crabtree, 2008.
Medina, Sarah. Sad (Feelings).
   Chicago: Heinemann Library, 2007.
Rosen, Michael. Michael Rosen's Sad Book.
   Cambridge, Mass.: Candlewick, 2005.

## Internet sites

Facthound offers a safe, fun way to find Internet sites related to this book. All of the sites on Facthound have been researched by our staff.

Here's all you do:
Visit www.facthound.com
Type in this code: 9781432971083

# Index